NOTE: ALL SCRIPTURES ARE QUOTED FROM
www.biblegateway.com

INTRODUCTION

As you read this book, have an open mind. Naaman was a king, he went to see prophet Elijah seeking for healing but he was disappointed. He went thinking there was a way his leprosy would get healed but he was challenged. He had to open his mind to the new way if he needed to see the healing he desired.

2nd kings 5:9-14

So Naaman went with his horses and chariots and stopped at the door of Elisha's house. **Elisha sent a messenger to say to him, "Go, wash yourself seven times in Jordan, and your flesh will be restored and you will be cleansed."** But Naaman went away angry and said, "I thought that he would surely come out to me and stand and call on the name of the Lord his God, wave his hand over the spot and

cure me of my leprosy.Are not Abana and Pharpar, the rivers of Damascus, better than all the waters of Israel? Couldn't I wash in them and be cleansed?" So he turned and went off in a rage.

 Naaman's servants went to him and said, "My father, if the prophet had told you to do some great thing, would you not have done it? How much more, then, when he tells you, 'Wash and be cleansed'!" So he went down and dipped himself in the Jordan seven times, as the man of God had told him, and his flesh was restored and became clean like that of a young boy.

People have a fixed way of thinking about how to make money but there is more and that needs a new mindset to receive it. Circumstances change but principles don't.

Isaiah 40:8
The grass withers and the flowers fall,
 but the word of our God endures forever."

CHAPTER ONE: WHAT IS MONEY
Real money is not the paper or coin you see, it's value. Value cannot be seen with the eyes. Before, people traded without money. They exchanged based on the values of the physical products they brought to the market. If you had potatoes then I brought tomatoes of the same value and we exchanged. It was tiresome and to make transactions easy, people invented money to represent the value of the physical products they had.

Today, you have to come to the market with something of value, exchange it and go home with money. Money becomes a means of exchange. Settle this in your heart, you will not get something for nothing. Bring what you have to the marketplace, be it skill, knowledge, products etc. Don't undermine what you have no matter how insignificant you consider it to be. The widow who was in debt undermined her oil in the house not knowing that little oil was going to get her out of poverty to be financially free.

2nd kings 4:1-7
The wife of a man from the company of the prophets cried out to Elisha, "Your servant my husband is dead, and you know that he revered the Lord. But now his creditor is coming to take my two boys as his slaves."
 Elisha replied to her, "How can I help you? Tell me, what do you have in your house?"
"Your servant has nothing there at all," she said, "except a small jar of olive oil."

Elisha said, "Go around and ask all your neighbours for empty jars. Don't ask for just a few.Then go inside and shut the door behind you and your sons. Pour oil into all the jars, and as each is filled, put it to one side."
She left him and shut the door behind her and her sons. They brought the jars to her and she kept pouring.When all the jars were full, she said to her son, "Bring me another one."
But he replied, "There is not a jar left." Then the oil stopped flowing.
She went and told the man of God, and he said, "Go, sell the oil and pay your debts. You and your sons can live on what is left."

I know we can pray, bind the devil and bury demons in coffins but when it comes to breaking free from poverty, understanding is needed.

CHAPTER TWO: WHAT GOD USED

Genesis 1:1-5

In the beginning God created the heavens and the earth.Now the earth was formless and empty, darkness was over the surface of the deep, and the Spirit of God was hovering over the waters. And God said, "Let there be light," and there was light. God saw that the light was good, and he separated the light from the darkness. God called the light "day," and the darkness he called "night." And there was evening, and there was morning— the first day.

In genesis verse 1, we are told God created the heavens and the earth but we are not given the raw material he used. However, in the following verses, we are given the raw material and it was "words."

Wealth is intangible.Those who value the intangible will get the tangible. The definition of wealth that many have is wrong. They see wealth only as tangible money. "How will we know your wealth has arrived if we don't see the house, car etc" They associate wealth with what is seen and if nothing, they call themselves or others poor. That thinking of majoring wealth on the physical has to change.

Hebrews 11:3
 By faith we understand that the universe was formed at God's command, so that what is seen was not made out of what was visible.

God used words to create the world and words are invisible. This offers a new thinking, value the invisible before it brings the visible and you will see yourself rich without any money in the bank yet.

That's an answer to those who say,"I can't do business because I don't have capital." God didn't use any capital to create the world, he valued the intangible and he saw them bring the tangible.

What the devil wants you to do is to see yourself as poor and incomplete without the material wealth. This kind of thinking he offers, if you take it, you will do anything to get the tangible money just to prove you are rich. The devil is the master of the natural realm.Eve fell for that trick and became worse than she was in the beginning,she lost the garden of eden. The devil tried to show her she was not like God and only eating the fruit will make her like God. She didn't value the intangible, the fact that God had said he had made man in his image, she was already like

God. In other words, she was trying to be what she already was.

Genesis 1-27
So God created man in his own image, in the image of God created he him; male and female created he them.

Genesis 3:5-7
For God knows that when you eat from it your eyes will be opened, and you will be like God, knowing good and evil."
When the woman saw that the fruit of the tree was good for food and pleasing to the eye, and also desirable for gaining wisdom, she took some and ate it. She also gave some to her husband, who was with her, and he ate it.Then the eyes of both of them were opened, and they realised they

were naked; so they sewed fig leaves together and made coverings for themselves.

Genesis 3:22-23
And the Lord God said, "The man has now become like one of us, knowing good and evil. He must not be allowed to reach out his hand and take also from the tree of life and eat, and live forever." So the Lord God banished him from the Garden of Eden to work the ground from which he had been taken.

You are not the poor trying to be rich, no! You are the rich one manifesting riches. That's a mindshifting statement. The materials don't define your value, it's the intangible that does. God says you are blessed and it's that intangible power that attracts wealth in your life. Start valuing the intangible wealth and you will see the tangible.

Ephesians 1:3
Praise be to the God and Father of our Lord
Jesus Christ, who has blessed us in the heavenly
realms with every spiritual blessing in Christ.

Proverbs 10:22
The blessing of the Lord makes one rich,
And He adds no sorrow with it.

Jesus didn't fall for Satan's trap. When the devil
tried to show him to prove his worth by changing
the stone into bread, he showed how he valued
the invisible which was God's word. He knew his
value was from the intangible world later to be
converted into the tangible. It was just a matter of
time and Jesus fed so many people by multiplying
bread and fish. Unlike Adam and Eve who didn't
have any value for the intangible and lost the

garden of Eden, Jesus valued the word of God which was intangible and he saw tangible wealth.

Matthew 4:3-4
After fasting forty days and forty nights, he was hungry.The tempter came to him and said, "If you are the Son of God, tell these stones to become bread."
 Jesus answered, "It is written: 'Man shall not live on bread alone, but on every word that comes from the mouth of God.'"

Matthew 14:15-21
As evening approached, the disciples came to him and said, "This is a remote place, and it's already getting late. Send the crowds away, so they can go to the villages and buy themselves some food."

Jesus replied, "They do not need to go away. You give them something to eat."

"We have here only five loaves of bread and two fish," they answered.

"Bring them here to me," he said. And he directed the people to sit down on the grass. Taking the five loaves and the two fish and looking up to heaven, he gave thanks and broke the loaves. Then he gave them to the disciples, and the disciples gave them to the people. They all ate and were satisfied, and the disciples picked up twelve basketfuls of broken pieces that were left over.The number of those who ate was about five thousand men, besides women and children.

CHAPTER THREE: VALUE THE INTANGIBLE

1: Words and thoughts

As you will think, so you will be. The quality of your thoughts determine the quality of your life.

Proverbs 23:7
For as he thinks in his heart, so is he.

God used words to create the world. Words come from thoughts. He saw the light, sun,moon, stars, animals, man, plants etc in his mind before he started speaking.Thoughts are intangible but they produce tangible things. Everything we see today, the cars, buildings, electronics, planes etc they were someones ideas. You have to pull off your religious goggles. You cannot see words or thoughts, but they have value. It's not the absence of money that makes people poor, it's the absence of value and value cannot be seen. Increase your value and increase your money. Don't joke with your capacity to think, that's why meditation is powerful and God wants his children to take time in his word so it changes their thinking. When they do so, they see, think, plan and talk like God.

Romans 12:2
Do not conform to the pattern of this world, but be transformed by the renewing of your mind. Then you will be able to test and approve what God's will is—his good, pleasing and perfect will.

Joshua 1:8
This Book of the Law shall not depart out of thy mouth, but thou shalt meditate therein day and night, that thou mayest observe to do according to all that is written therein. For then thou shalt make thy way prosperous, and then thou shalt have good success.

As you meditate on the word of God, the holy spirit gives you ideas, thoughts and plans that if you implement, they can take you out of poverty.

Proverbs 21:5
The thoughts of the diligent tend only to plenteousness, but of everyone that is hasty, only to want.

2: Time
They say time is money. Those who know how to manage time end up wealthy. God is not a waster and wasting time will lead to poverty. The just God gave all people 24 hours in a day, how they use it it's their choice. God is the maker of both the rich and the poor but he never made them rich or poor, how they use the resources he made available is their choice.

Psalms 104:19
He appointed the moon for seasons: the sun
knoweth his going down.

Proverbs 22:2
Rich and poor have this in common:
 The Lord is the Maker of them all.

3: Association
The people you interact with, transfer their ideas
and belief systems to you. What they transfer to
you is invisible but soon it will be seen. They can
give you thoughts of poverty or prosperity.

Proverbs 27:17
As iron sharpens iron,
    so one person sharpens another.

Psalms 1:3

Blessed is the man who does not walk in step
with the wicked
or stand in the way that sinners take
or sit in the company of mockers,
but whose delight is in the law of the Lord,
and who meditates on his law day and night.
That person is like a tree planted by streams of
water,
which yields its fruit in season
and whose leaf does not wither—
whatever they do prospers.

4: Integrity

These are values and principles adopted as
personal standard. The less you trust someone,
the less money you are willing to commit to
him/her. People who have created a track record,
are easily trustworthy. In the parable of the
talents, the man that proved trustworthy with little

received double and the unfaithful got all taken from him.

Luke 16:10
He that is faithful in that which is least, is faithful also in much; and he that is unjust in the least, is unjust also in much.

Matthew 25:14-30
For it will be like a man going on a journey, who called his servants and entrusted to them his property. To one he gave five talents,to another two, to another one, to each according to his ability. Then he went away.He who had received the five talents went at once and traded with them, and he made five talents more. So also he who had the two talents made two talents more.But he who had received the one talent went and dug in the ground and hid his master's

money. Now after a long time the master of those servants came and settled accounts with them. And he who had received the five talents came forward, bringing five talents more, saying, 'Master, you delivered to me five talents; here, I have made five talents more.'His master said to him, 'Well done, good and faithful servant.You have been faithful over a little; I will set you over much. Enter into the joy of your master.' And he also who had the two talents came forward, saying, 'Master, you delivered to me two talents; here, I have made two talents more.'His master said to him, 'Well done, good and faithful servant. You have been faithful over a little; I will set you over much. Enter into the joy of your master.' He also who had received the one talent came forward, saying, 'Master, I knew you to be a hard man, reaping where you did not sow, and gathering where you scattered no seed,so I was afraid, and I went and hid your talent in the ground. Here, you have what is yours.' But his master answered him, 'You wicked and slothful servant! You knew that I reap where I have not sown and gather where I scattered no seed? Then you ought to have invested my money with the bankers, and at my coming I should have received what was my own with interest. So take the talent from him and give it to him who has the ten talents. For to everyone who has will more be given, and he will have an abundance. But from the one who has not, even what he has will be taken away. And cast the worthless servant into the outer darkness. In that place there will be weeping and gnashing of teeth.'

5: The Blessing
What God gave to Adam and Eve was not money but the blessing. His power to make them

wealthy. From all God made, they could not reproduce and recreate. Adam and Eve had the power to bring another child just like them and today the whole world is full of people. From trees people can now make furnitures, houses etc.

Genesis 1:28
God blessed them and said to them, "Be fruitful and increase in number; fill the earth and subdue it. Rule over the fish in the sea and the birds in the sky and over every living creature that moves on the ground."

Jacob knew the power of this intangible blessing, he was willing to trade his soup to get it.

Gensis 25:29-34
Once when Jacob was cooking stew, Esau came in from the field, and he was exhausted.And Esau

said to Jacob, "Let me eat some of that red stew, for I am exhausted!" (Therefore his name was called Edom.Jacob said, "**Sell me your birthright now." Esau said, "I am about to die; of what use is a birthright to me?" Jacob said, "Swear to me now." So he swore to him and sold his birthright to Jacob.**Then Jacob gave Esau bread and lentil stew, and he ate and drank and rose and went his way. Thus Esau despised his birthright.

 Understand and value the blessing of God in your life and you will see it bring the tangible. Don't be like Esau who despised the invisible and was left with tears later. Value the intangible and the tangible will come. If you sell products, ensure they are of value for you to get good money. If you offer things of low value, you will get little money.

Esau when he lost the chance to be blessed cried alot and with time, the blessing made Jacob so rich.

Hebrews 12:16-17
like Esau, who sold his birthright for a single meal. For you know that afterward, when he desired to inherit the blessing, he was rejected, for he found no chance to repent, though he sought it with tears.

Genesis 27:28
Esau said to his father, Have you only one blessing, my father? Bless me, even me also, O my father! And Esau lifted up [could not control] his voice and wept aloud.

Genesis 30:43

As a result, Jacob became very wealthy, with large flocks of sheep and goats, female and male servants, and many camels and donkeys.

When God called Abraham, he gave him the blessing and he had the power to get so much wealth.

Genesis 12:1-3
The Lord had said to Abram, "Go from your country, your people and your father's household to the land I will show you.

 "I will make you into a great nation,
  and I will bless you;
I will make your name great,
  and you will be a blessing.
I will bless those who bless you,
  and whoever curses you I will curse;

and all peoples on earth
   will be blessed through you."

Genesis 13:2
And Abram was very rich in cattle, in silver, and in gold.

6: The presence of God
God's presence which is intangible attracts the visible in your life. Jesus said seek first the kingdom and his righteousness which are invisible and all the material will be added. What he didn't put straight was that he is the king of the kingdom and our righteousness. Therefore, spending time with him is not a waste but another advantage to getting the tangible.

Matthew 6:25-34

"Therefore I tell you, do not worry about your life, what you will eat or drink; or about your body, what you will wear. Is not life more than food, and the body more than clothes? Look at the birds of the air; they do not sow or reap or store away in barns, and yet your heavenly Father feeds them. Are you not much more valuable than they? Can any one of you by worrying add a single hour to your life?

"And why do you worry about clothes? See how the flowers of the field grow. They do not labor or spin. Yet I tell you that not even Solomon in all his splendor was dressed like one of these. If that is how God clothes the grass of the field, which is here today and tomorrow is thrown into the fire, will he not much more clothe you—you of little faith? So do not worry, saying, 'What shall we eat?' or 'What shall we drink?' or 'What shall we wear?' For the pagans run after all these things, and your heavenly Father knows that you need them. But seek first his kingdom and his righteousness, and all these things will be given to you as well. Therefore do not worry about tomorrow, for tomorrow will worry about itself. Each day has enough trouble of its own.

7: Favour
God's favour is intangible but it produces tangible results. God gave the Israelites favour that the Egyptians gave them all they had.

Exodus 12:36
The Lord gave the people favour in the sight of the Egyptians, so that they gave them what they asked. And so they plundered the Egyptians [of those things].

God gave Esther the intangible favour but it brought her to the throne as a queen.

Esther 2:17
Now the king was attracted to Esther more than to any of the other women, and she won his favour and approval more than any of the other virgins. So he set a royal crown on her head and made her queen instead of Vashti.

8: Gifts
Talents and gifts are invisible but they produce visible results. Identify your gifts and talents and use them to get money.

Proverbs 18:16
 A man's gift maketh room for him, and bringeth him before great men.

Proverbs 22:29
Do you see a person skilled in his work? He will stand in the presence of kings. He will not stand in the presence of the unknown.

CHAPTER FOUR: HOW GOD GIVES YOU MONEY

Your mind also changes about prayers. When you ask God for money, there is no money in heaven. I know that has shocked some people. You have to know how God gives you money. The answer God gives you is revelation, his word, light, ideas.

Psalms 107:20
He sent His word and healed them,
And saved them from their destruction.

Psalms 119:105
Thy word is a lamp unto my feet, and a light unto my path.

As you pray or after praying, God sends his word to you in the form of an instruction, idea or thought. Take that word and act on it and it will bring you what you need.

John 1:14
The Word became flesh and made his dwelling among us. We have seen his glory, the glory of the one and only Son, who came from the Father, full of grace and truth.

Most Christians ignore that since it doesn't agree with their belief system and they continue to pray not knowing the answer came a long time ago.

Others like Peter give excuses as to why the word can't work. But the word of God created the world, it never fails for all things are made by the word.

Hebrews 1:3
Who being the brightness of his glory, and the express image of his person, and upholding all things by the word of his power.

Luke 5:4-6
When he had finished speaking, he said to Simon, "Put out into deep water, and let down the nets for a catch."
Simon answered, "Master, we've worked hard all night and haven't caught anything. But because you say so, I will let down the nets."
When they had done so, they caught such a large number of fish that their nets began to

break.So they signalled their partners in the other boat to come and help them, and they came and filled both boats so full that they began to sink.

The devil knows how God answers and he makes sure immediately God releases the word, revelations, instruction, idea or thoughts, he steals it.

Matthew 13:8-9
"Listen then to what the parable of the sower means: When anyone hears the message about the kingdom and does not understand it, **the evil one comes and snatches away what was sown in their heart.** This is the seed sown along the path.

Many do like the Christians in acts did, they pray for peter not knowing Peter has already been released and he is at their door. When told Peter is outside, they say it's his angle and continue with the prayers.

Acts 12:1-16
It was about this time that King Herod arrested some who belonged to the church, intending to persecute them.He had James, the brother of John, put to death with the sword. When he saw that this met with approval among the Jews, he proceeded to seize Peter also. This happened during the Festival of Unleavened Bread.After arresting him, he put him in prison, handing him over to be guarded by four squads of four soldiers each. Herod intended to bring him out for public trial after the Passover.

So Peter was kept in prison, but the church was earnestly praying to God for him.
The night before Herod was to bring him to trial, Peter was sleeping between two soldiers, bound with two chains, and sentries stood guard at the entrance. **Suddenly an angel of the Lord appeared and a light shone in the cell. He struck Peter on the side and woke him up. "Quick, get up!" he said, and the chains fell off Peter's wrists.**

Then the angel said to him, "Put on your clothes and sandals." And Peter did so. "Wrap your cloak around you and follow me," the angel told him. Peter followed him out of the prison, but he had no idea that what the angel was doing was really happening; he thought he was seeing a vision. They passed the first and second guards and came to the iron gate leading to the city. It opened for them by itself, and they went through it. When they had walked the length of one street, suddenly the angel left him.

Then Peter came to himself and said, "Now I know without a doubt that the Lord has sent his angel and rescued me from Herod's clutches and from everything the Jewish people were hoping would happen."

When this had dawned on him, he went to the house of Mary the mother of John, also called Mark, where many people had gathered and were praying. Peter knocked at the outer entrance, and a servant named Rhoda came to answer the door. When she recognized Peter's voice, she was so overjoyed she ran back without opening it and exclaimed, "Peter is at the door!"

"You're out of your mind," they told her. When she kept insisting that it was so, they said, "It must be his angel."

But Peter kept on knocking, and when they opened the door and saw him, they were astonished. Peter motioned with his hand for them to be quiet and described how the Lord had brought him out of prison. "Tell James and the other brothers and sisters about this," he said, and then he left for another place.

Take time and recall all the ideas and promises God gave you that you had ignored, despised or seen as impossible and write them down for they will be your vision. You will be amazed that your provision is in your vision.

Habakkuk 2:1-3
I will stand at my watch
   and station myself on the ramparts;
I will look to see what he will say to me,
   and what answer I am to give to this complaint.

Then the Lord replied:

"Write down the revelation
    and make it plain on tablets
    so that a herald may run with it.
For the revelation awaits an appointed time;
    it speaks of the end
    and will not prove false.
Though it linger, wait for it;
    it will certainly come
    and will not delay.

Proverbs 29:18
Where there is no vision, the people perish: but
he that keepeth the law, happy is he.

2nd corinthians 1:20

For as many as are the promises of God, in Christ they are [all answered] "Yes." So through Him we say our "Amen" to the glory of God.

www.ingramcontent.com/pod-product-compliance
Lightning Source LLC
Chambersburg PA
CBHW071146220526
45467CB00015B/1990